To all the women struggling to let go, searching for their self-worth, or settling for an imitation of love, I hope you find understanding and are encouraged by the wisdom splattered on each page with my love. Know that you are not alone and that letting go is a process that ends in a peaceful place.

PRESSING PAST THE PAIN

Volume 1

Cioré Taylor

Published By: SquareKnot Resources LLC

Copyright © 2017 Cioré Taylor
All rights reserved.

ISBN-10:
0-9986352-0-0

ISBN-13:
978-0-9986352-0-0

TABLE OF CONTENTS

Introduction	6
1. You Are Not Alone	8
2. Hard Lessons Learnt	21
3. Learning to Let Go	33
4. Slowly Moving Forward	45
5. Embracing the Wait	56
6. A Moment of Doubt	67
7. Encourage Yourself	79
8. You've Got This	90
9. My Pledge	101

INTRODUCTION

Many people will look at our lives and recommend the book they FEEL is best suited for what they THINK we are going through. However, people can only see so much of the lives we live and if we do not welcome them to be a part of our solution, then the advice they think we need may not even offer answers remotely relevant to the questions we have or the challenges we are facing. Many of the books start from chapter one giving advice and the reader's entire experience is one way. This is not that type of book! I do not want you to feel like I am talking *at* you or as if I am preaching to the choir. I WANT you to feel my desire to work WITH you. I WANT you to be involved and to feel empowered every step of the way. I want you to witness the moment your paradigm changes. I want this book to serve as a reminder of the very second the light clicked in your mind and you were able to envision a future better than your past. Don't be afraid to be honest with yourself. Transparency is key to unlocking the hidden power that lies within you! Be encouraged and allow this book to bless you as it invites you to have a much needed conversation with yourself.

Chapter 1
YOU ARE NOT ALONE

Baby, dry those eyes. Some people aren't worthy of your tears.

Some nights we may want to cry because loneliness overwhelms us and the thought of sleeping alone depresses us, but we must wipe our eyes and save our tears for the moments of joy that deserve them. We have to stop crying over situations we know brought us more bad than good. We have to stop shedding tears because we feel misunderstood. They understood. They may not have cared, they may not have recognized when they were doing it or they may not have loved us enough to make the intentional change but they knew what they were doing when they hurt us. Every tear we shed entertains the idea that maybe just maybe it could have worked if we coulda woulda shoulda. Stop that crazy talk. Stop entertaining foolishness. Save your tears for situations worthy of them. You are strong. You are unbreakable. You are a child of the most high and nothing will destroy you. Walk in the confidence of knowing that you will not be defeated. You WILL make it through this day and you WILL sleep in peace tonight.

It may not seem like it now, but you're going to get through this. I pray peace to your situation, faith through limited understanding and joy for the victory that has already been won. God is in control.

You are going to get through this, just know that God is in control. God sees your tears and your pain, and when you are hurting, He is hurting. The enemy tries to create a hell that God did not put you in and God wants to rescue you from that illusion. His desire is that his children find peace and contentment in him in EVERY situation. He is a way maker. He is an ever present help in the time of trouble and He always wins. As you go through a breakup, a job transition or a period of loneliness or depression, God is there. Not only is he there to fight on your behalf but he is there to give you a peace beyond your understanding. He is there to give you joy beyond reason. God is there to show you that the love you are looking for is within Him. You don't have to want for anything because there's nothing He can't give you. Keep your head up and trust that as long as God is in control, you are going to be okay.

To be rejected from situations unfit for you is natural, to feel rejection is the enemy's work.

I promise, rejection is the work of the enemy. God may allow some things to be kept away from us for our own good because we are not ready for them, poor timing or because He just wants to say no. However, that feeling of "Why me, God", "I'm never going to get through this", "Nobody's knows what I'm going through" type of feeling; that's the enemy trying to make us feel unworthy. It's his job to make us feel small and undeserving. He wants us to feel we are alone in our struggles so that we will turn to anger, depression, hate, violence, bitterness, jealousy and meaningless sex. He wants us to demean ourselves so our expected reaction is to fall into another cycle of hopelessness and despair, creating voids so large in our hearts that we cannot even remember what it was like to feel accepted. Rejection is a strong source of pain that we can choose not to let control our lives. We can choose to see our situation differently and choose to move forward knowing that if God denied it then He must have something better in store.

The longer we hold on to baggage, the heavier it gets.

I think we all know how this message applies with literal baggage, but did you know that it also applies with emotional baggage. For example, when we are carrying our suitcase through the airport or at the bus station, its weight feels manageable in the beginning. As long as we keep moving, we barely notice how heavy our luggage actually is. It's when the hustle and bustle is over that we begin to realize how much weight we are actually carrying. Not only do we realize how heavy it is, but we also realize that the longer we hold it, the heavier it gets. This realization also happens when we stop floating through the new stages of a relationship and begin to focus on what's real. The truth is that some relationships are not meant to be. The longer we hold on to the people we are ready to let go of, the harder it gets to hold on to them because of how heavy the burden becomes. The weight of the truth begins to bring us down and we feel weakened in the fight to hold on to foolishness. Fortunately for us, the best part of carrying baggage is the moment we get to unpack it. No more strain, no more stress, no more baggage. Maybe you have some baggage you want to let go, but can't quite convince yourself to do it. You just need to ask yourself, is it worth the strain?

"The truth is that some relationships are not meant to be."

You are stronger than you think you are.

Keep fighting.

Are feeling weak today? Stressed? Overwhelmed? Tired of work? Tired of school? Take a deep breath. You WILL conquer this day, and it will not defeat you. You are stronger than you think you are. Keep your head up. You are not alone. You will never be alone. Even on your loneliest days, God is there and he wants to comfort you. He wants to encourage you. He wants to love on you and put a smile on your face. He is willing to turn your situation around and be all that you need him to be. He only desires that you let him into your life so he can begin to clean up the mess in heart and rebuild what has been destroyed. Let him love on you today. Do not stress or worry about how you are going to get through this. God is going to carry you through, that's how. You just have to keep fighting.

Don't allow your situation to BREAK you before you allow God to CHANGE you.

It's a new day and a new opportunity to improve yourself, your situation, and your mindset. Do not be resistant to change, with change comes new possibilities. The possibilities in your life are limitless and it all starts with you. It begins with you seeing a lesson in every struggle and an opportunity in every detour. There are many things in our lives that are out of our control but it's not our job to become upset over the challenges life throws at us. Our responsibility is to look at our life and say, "No matter what you try to throw at me, I know God is in control and He will make a way for me," However, you cannot just say this, you have to believe it and know it to be true. The moment we confess with our hearts we are going to trust God, even when we don't understand, is the moment God has the opportunity to bless our lives and change us for the better. It's easy to be overwhelmed by some of the negativity thrown our way but the moment we realize that God is our shield we can live in freedom knowing we have nothing to fear because God will protect us. Therefore, do not be afraid. Know that God is with you and that today you have the opportunity to be great.

Moment of Reflection:

Are you ready and willing to embrace positive change in your life and why?

_____
_____
_____
_____
_____
_____
_____
_____

Sometimes... your man, your friends and your girlfriends just won't get it, but you must KEEP IT MOVING.

The road to success is lonely and most people will often misunderstand what you are doing or where it is you are trying to go. We can't let the thought of feeling lonely wait to discourage us from moving forward in life. The truth is, when people don't understand where you came from, they cannot comprehend the distance you have endured to achieve your dream. Sometimes, they know where you came from but still don't know how to support you. We cannot become upset with the people we love because they don't understand the goals we are trying to reach. We can only pray God will bring like-minded people in our lives who can genuinely celebrate the large and small victories with us. Until then, we have to keep on keeping on and trust that we will be okay. We never know who's watching us, looking to learn from us, hoping that they can do what we do. Be aware your time is coming where somebody is going to understand you and be willing to support you the correct way.

Sometimes it takes going through some things to be able to appreciate some things. It's a process.

Do not be ashamed of your process, we all have one. It's not our mistakes that define us but it's how we manage our process of overcoming those mistakes. It's our ability to see our future past our insecurities and to transform our lives into better versions of ourselves that matters. We are not striving to be perfect versions of ourselves but BETTER versions of ourselves. Be encouraged!

"Be encouraged."

Sometimes you have to sacrifice the one you want for the one who wants to love you right.

In a mere moment, letting go can be hard and can feel like it's never going to work, but something tells me if we stick to loving ourselves and focus on developing our future, we are going to be glad we waited for love to find us. Can you imagine living the life you were meant to live, one hundred percent content with where God has led you and then, when you least expect it, God drops an angel out of heaven to protect your heart for the rest of your life? Can you image a life so beautiful with a man that you do not have to teach him how to love you but with a man who walked into your life ready to love you? Having an imagination is God's gift to us. He gives us the mind to see what is possible and in return we must explore it regularly, strengthening our faith toward what can be. There's nothing impossible for God and it requires faith to really know what that looks like. You may have little faith now, but I pray God fills your life with reassurance He is present in your life. Love is in front of you, just wait for it.

God wants us to stop chasing after an imperfect love and to start chasing after Him, the one who makes imperfect love perfect.

We all want to be loved therefore God allows us to see through all of our failed relationships that He doesn't just want us to experience any kind of love, He wants us to experience love the right way. God wants us to understand how He loves us so perfectly and how He is the one who can make imperfect love perfect. There are times we are so busy looking backward that we neglect to see the purest version of love he shows us every day. You may have stayed in a relationship so long that you began to believe love existed there when really it did not. Sometimes the love you are chasing actually isn't love at all but it is control, lust, manipulation or an insecurity. When we pursue God first, He will show us what love really is with God on our side, we will never have to settle. We just need to be patient. Be encouraged.

Chapter 2
HARD LESSONS LEARNT

If they couldn't see the real you with the lights on, why did you let them touch you with the lights off?

This is a very serious question that can be quite easy to ask, but sometimes hard to answer. Many of us are caught up in soul ties because we give our goodies away to someone who did not deserve them. We attempt to love people by giving them our all knowing they do not know how to appreciate it. For so many of us, we have been giving ourselves away to others as if we weren't worthy to be the prize of their lives. Because we did not value ourselves the way that we should of, it slowly became hard for us to know when we were being treated like trash. We all learn eventually that we are worthy of more than disrespect, one night stands and unfaithfulness. Some of us have to learn the hard way. The important thing is that we apply what we learn to bettering ourselves in the future. If we don't want to repeat the past, then we have to act differently. Change requires commitment, so you willing to commit to changing your habits to create a better future? The choice is yours.

If he doesn't respect it, he won't protect it.

Does he respect you, your character, your body, your family, or your relationship with God? Does he respect it enough to fight for it? If the answer is no, are you strong enough to fight for it alone? The answer is yes. You are strong enough to fight your battles alone and therefore, no, you don't need him. But why fight alone if you don't have to? Why feel alone if you don't have to? Why feel disrespected if you don't have to? Why feel insecure in your relationship? Why feel unappreciated? You are worthy of so much more than unhappy endings and living a life of fear. You deserve to have a sound mind. You deserve to live in peace. You deserve to be loved. You deserve to be led by someone who understands you. Don't settle for disrespect. Also don't settle for uncertainty. He may not be a bad guy, but if you don't feel secure with him you can definitely do better. Do what's best for you, no matter what the perception is because God's is watching over you. If there is one person who will always protect you, it's him. Remember that when you think you won't make it on your own. God always has your back.

Sometimes the hardest part about learning the truth is that you rid yourself of all excuses to keep going back.

Those who know better do better, or at least they try to do better. It may get hard, but if you don't try how will you ever discover the strength within you. You are worthy of so much more than the games, the lies and deceit. Your value is worth much more than some individual seeking other options while they are with you. You are a prize. You are a queen. Take pride in who God has created you to be. Take pride in the conqueror living inside of you that ensures you can make it through anything. Love yourself enough to stay focused moving forward. Turning back is not an option. You can do this.

He told her everything ain't for everybody, so she took her heart back to prove it.

Sometimes you have to do what you have to do. Don't ask any questions, just take what's yours and go. When people don't care, it's not that they don't want to, it's just they do not know how to love you right. For the man who has never been taught to love correctly, it's possible they don't even know when they are devaluing you. They may think yelling at you is okay because they saw their father do it to their mom. They may think calling you to see where you are every five minutes is a man's job because they saw it in movies. Some men aren't gentle because gentleness was never exposed to them. For these reasons, when men make you choose between tolerating their mess and loving yourself, you must choose yourself. You must find strength in yourself and recall what is most important in life. It's crucial to live your life and to pursue the greatness that is within you. If they are constantly challenging what you deserve or interfering with your progress, then please, do what you need to do and prioritize you. You will be better for it.

They thought the relationship was good while it lasted but I was still waiting on everything to get better.

It's times like this when you need to let go, especially when you are bending over backwards to illustrate your hurt, loneliness and desire for more. Your need for more is misunderstood and all they hear you say is "everything is fine." You need someone who listens and hears you, who learns from their mistakes and apply themselves towards your history together. Feeling alone in a relationship is not fun and when you spend months to years trying to reverse that feeling the truth remains, sometimes it's just time to let go. Asking why may only yield more unanswered questions. Don't let curiosity be the reason you stay in a relationship. There needs to be substance. Ultimately the decision is yours. The question is, will you make the right one?

Sometimes the hardest part of letting go of Mr. Wrong is that not all of you all's memories were bad.

Many of us know this feeling all too well so I'm going to keep it simple. We decide who we allow to stay in our lives and it's up to us to decide if their presence will result in a better or worse future for ourselves. If we don't choose wisely, we only have ourselves to blame. If we want to become better than we have to be committed to doing better. The power to be great is inside of everyone, but we hide it because we are afraid to let go; as a result, we end up denying ourselves the opportunities God wants to give us. Stay because you want to… because you love them… because you believe you two are meant to be. Don't stay because you are under the assumption things MIGHT get better. You have to realize that you are strong enough to walk away from situations that don't bring out the best in you. Maybe one day you two will be in a different place in life and have the opportunity to reminisce over the past, but today is not that day. Today you have to get back to focusing on yourself.

This time when he decided to walk away, I shut the door behind him.

When you leave the door to your heart open, you increase the chance for anyone to rob you of your love. When you don't protect the value you withhold, you tell the world, you aren't worth the fight. You tell the world you are not worth appreciation. You are worthy of appreciation and God's army of angels. You are THAT special. Protect your love because it's priceless to the one who is patiently searching for it. Those who can't appreciate the worth you possess, are not qualified to handle it. This is a truth you can trust. Shut the door and turn on the alarm when men walk away from your life. You are a good thing and your love is a sure thing. Those temporarily passing through are not welcome to enter as they please. Make sure the next person knows the value of what's inside of you before you give them access.

You can love them through it all, but if they do not know what love is, it will never be enough.

Sometimes you have to accept the truth, try to swallow your pride and do your best to move on. Wondering why your love did not work is a futile exercise that yields no benefits. Love is simple when shared the right way but it gets complicated when neither person understands how to express it. You see, you can think you are loving them right, but if they don't understand your love then they can't appreciate it. If they don't appreciate your love, what good is that? The same way they can't understand your love, you constantly feel like they don't love you. They may be loving you the way they witnessed "love" in their childhood but because you totally disagree with the way that they express it, you won't accept it. Your love is not enough for them and their love is not enough for you. Stressing out over why you two cannot figure it out does not help to solve the problem, it only adds more confusion to the problem. Take a step back and realize that you two are missing something. You two are missing the glue that makes happily ever after work. Both of you do not have a mutual standard of love that you are working toward and therefore, someone will always be dissatisfied. Satisfaction does exist for you, but you have to be willing to wait for it while you move forward pursuing your best you. Are you willing to wait?

Moment of Reflection:
Are you willing to wait?

When your convictions start to get stronger about the things you have been doing wrong, get excited, because it means that you are finally on track to start doing things right.

The moment you start thinking twice about what has become second nature to you, is the moment you are on the cusp of change. Your breakthrough is so close; you are literally beginning to feel it. Don't be afraid to transform into a better you. Your whole body is preparing itself for a change within you and that is why you feel it in your gut when you are doing something you have no business doing. It doesn't have to even be anything major. Maybe you are thinking twice about gossiping or hanging out with the group of friends who don't add value to your life. Maybe you are thinking twice about lying, cheating, stealing, yelling, fighting, being bitter all time or reaching out to that long lost love. Whatever the case is, you already know what you need to fix. A part of you already wants to fix it and that's why you are thinking twice. Don't resist the change, just wait for it to happen! You'll be blown away with who you discover you can be. Be encouraged.

A relationship without a vision of the future will soon become a story of the past.

If you can't imagine yourself being with them in the future, or if the thought of still being with them in the future makes you cringe, you might as well make them a part of your past. It's the best thing for both of you and you have already started to realize it. The beauty of relationships is imagining what you two can be together. I know I want to build an empire with the man made for me and I know that it is totally possible. However, building an empire is the future I imagine. It's a possibility that I know that God can make happen and I trust that it is already in his plan for me. It's when we fail to imagine the future that we settle for the option in front of us. Settling for Mr. Wrong is the wrong thing to do. It requires excessive misery, expensive life lessons and the hand of God to turn it around. Don't commit to going down the wrong road when all signs point to chaos. Pay attention to the signs, redirect your heart and choose to go down a different path. You can do it. Trust yourself.

Chapter 3
LEARNING TO LET GO

Your BEST resides in your future but you have to let go of the LESS in your past in order to get to it.

It's hard to imagine more in your future when you only know the life you have lived, but we can't let our past hold us back. If we want more then we have to be willing to let go of less in order to get it. Less may seem like all there is now but those who are willing to take the risk of letting go now to find out what more is in the future are the ones who win. It's time to go get our best. No more holding on to damaged goods.

"We deserve better."

Umm... No, we can't still be friends.

Let's stop trying to convince ourselves that we can still be friends with the people we JUST decided were not good for us. The answer is no we can't still be friends. The answer is no we cannot try to make this work just in case one of us changes our minds. The answer is no we cannot keep making the same mistakes hoping that things are going to change. We will not be reliving the past in confusion; we are either together or we are not. We can't uncross lines and we can't create new strict friend boundaries. It doesn't work like that and we know it. Being friends is not an option for us. My only option is to move forward trying to do better and be better.

Don't beg your way back into situations that it required the strength of God to walk away from.

I know it hurts. I know how hard it is to be still when it feels like you are losing control. I know how hard it can be to believe there is a purpose for your pain. Romans 8:28 says, "All things work together for good to those who love God and that are called according to his purpose." God is not allowing you to work through your struggle of finding contentment in Him for no reason. He is creating a testimony in you. Others who know you will have no other choice but to give Him the glory for all the love he wants to shower on you. Stay prayerful and stay faithful and when you get weak and don't go back. Continue forward in process. Remember that God sees you, all your hurts and all your pain, he sees it and desires that you give it to him. You are not alone.

Indecision is a decision and a bad habit that needs to be broken.

If you decide to walk away, then stay away. Don't go back in a moment of weakness, you are stronger than that. You just have to remember you are strong when you feel weak or you're never going to access the strength God wants to give you. I know it's hard but keep your head up. When you keep going back to the very thing that hurt you, that's insanity. When you cannot decide whether to you want to be happy or stay where you're at, that is indecision. You know what you want. You know what you deserve. Don't try to talk yourself out of what is best for you. That is a bad habit that needs to be broken and you can break it. Trust yourself. Trust your instincts. Trust your desire for more because you deserve it.

> **T**he longer you entertain soul ties, the tighter those knots get and the harder it is to loose yourself from situationships that should be a part of your past and not your future.

Soul ties are real. They are a spiritual bond that connect man and woman when those two engage in sexual intercourse. These bonds can get so strong that each partner literally becomes an extension of the other person. When one person hurts, they both hurt. When one person has anger issues, the other may find themselves more irritated each day for no reason. When two people have sex, their souls become connected and even when one tries to walk away, they are still connected. Soul ties can be broken through patience, separation and healing but they only get stronger when we entertain relationships with partners from our past. Now how are you going to feel after God blesses you with the one you've been waiting for but you can't enjoy the fire between you and Mr. Right because you are still fanning the old flames burning with Mr. Wrong. Old flames that are distracting you from your dream come true. Don't mess up your future blessings by entertaining relationships from the past out of loneliness or weakness. You're stronger than that.

Moment of Reflection:
Are you willing to wait?

_____
_____
_____
_____
_____
_____
_____
_____
_____
_____
_____

"You don't owe them anything."

For everyone staying in situations longer than you want, with someone you don't want to be with, just because you feel a sense of obligation to them for something they did for you in the past. Listen up, everyone is responsible for their own actions and we all make our own choices. If they helped you then it was because they wanted to and they made that decision. No matter who influenced their decision, they made it for themselves. What does this mean? It means you don't own them anything! If you are ready to let them go and walk away, do so confidently trusting that you have to do what's best for you. Walking away is apart of loving yourself, even if it may be hard. You can do it. Be encouraged!

Sooner or later, you are going to have to let go... all the way.

We can't keep fighting to avoid the truth. Letting go isn't easy and it will never happen if we keep holding on, even if we are just holding on to a little bit, the time to let go is now.

I was reminded tonight that just because you are doing okay without someone, doesn't mean you're completely willing to let them go. Sometimes we can wrap our minds around not talking on the phone to someone every day but when it comes to never speaking to our ex again, it seems impossible. I'm so guilty of this.

However, the time to let go is now! Not when you're ready and not when he's done entertaining the thoughts of being back together, but NOW! Prolonging this event will only leave you confused and seeking closure that doesn't exist in the package you want it. We have to remember that we are worthy of someone we can cherish and who will cherish us back. We are worthy of the greatest love and we are capable of doing so much better for ourselves than we imagine. Letting go is never easy, but WE can do this!!

When you find yourself, you will be less worried about losing him.

When you know who you are you will realize that he does not define you. You can define you, God can define you, but never let a man define you. He can support you, encourage you, compliment you and even be your other half. He can be the man of your dreams and the one you waited for, but even then, you will still define you. You choose if you will live according to his standards or according to God's standard. God wants you to be your best version of you and you can be that person. You can be at your best with the one who God has for you as well. Don't settle for the person you know is not for you in an attempt to find yourself. You don't have to do that. You just have to be patient and wait on God's best for you.

Don't be afraid to start over. This is your opportunity to right your wrongs and to unleash the greatness that lives within you!

Don't be discouraged that you're not where you want to be. Don't be frustrated that you have spent the past month or 6 months to 3 years guiding your life in the wrong direction. Take a depth breath, wash your face and put a good mood on. Everyone has to start from somewhere and that's just a part of life. Starting over isn't something to be embarrassed about, be thankful you're doing it now and it's not too late. Today you have the opportunity to rebuild yourself and your world the way you want to experience it and the way you want to be remembered. Keep your head up. You got this!

> "There's nothing that I need that God hasn't given and there's nothing good that I desire that God isn't preparing for me. Everything happens in God's timing."

Life can stress you out. Failed relationships can stress you out. Depression can steal your joy and you can become the pitiful person that you dread. Don't become that person. Hold your head up high and speak these words over your life. Know that even when life knocks you down, you will always be strong enough to pray for yourself and your situation. You are strong, beautiful and worthy of everything that God has for you. If you feel weak, don't give up but speak up. Remind yourself that this is the hardest part but you will get through this. Activate your faith and never forget, the only person you need in this life is the very one, God, who is helping you through this, not the man who left you.

Chapter 4
SLOWLY MOVING FORWARD

I thought I was over him but then I started drinking.

Moral of the story, don't drink. I'd add a smiley face here if I could to indicate to you that this is a joke, but seriously, transparency is key to you improving yourself. If in the moments that you are under the influence, you get drawn back into the memories of what used to be, you may realize that you have more work to do. The awesome thing is you do not have to act on the thoughts you are thinking. No matter the influence, you are in control of you. Do not try to blame your actions on the alcohol, it's you. Let's move forward in continued strength and honesty, knowing that no matter what our memories remind us, our actions will represent our best intentions and our commitment to moving forward.

Eventually, you'll get tired of settling for less than you deserve and you'll decide to do something about it, until then, you'll keep hurting because you refuse to help yourself.

At some time, we all get to the point where we've had enough of making bad choices. We all get to a point that we get tired of making excuses and hiding behind lies. Who doesn't want to live freely? Who doesn't want to feel comfort openly living the truth about who they are? We all want to be accepted whether that's for stuff we have in common or in ways that we differ. No one wants to live bound by poor choices. Unfortunately, some of just keep digging the hole we are living in because we are scared to walk into our own truth. Hopefully too many of us won't wait until it's too late to turn it around. No need to keep hurting for something that can be corrected. It definitely will not be easy, but what worth having ever is easy?

Don't let the thought of them having fun without you keep you from having fun alone.

It's hard to imagine more in our future when we only know the life we have lived, but we can't let our past hold us back. If we want more, then we have to be willing to let go of less. Less may seem like all there is now but those who are willing to take the risk letting go now to find out what more is in the future are the ones who win. It's time to find our best. No more holding on to damaged goods.

"We deserve better."

> **I**nstead of pursuing love in the wrong places, I'm going to pursue meaningful relationships with those who can help me achieve my purpose in life and develop a better me.

Where could we be if we focused on the life in front of us rather than the love that hasn't found us yet? I wonder. We spend so much time looking for something that we want without preparing ourselves to receive it when that time comes. We do not have to be anxious for anything. God knows what we want. Our job is not to tell the Lord how to do his job in our lives and which man to send us. Our job is to focus on being the best we can be so that we don't miss out on the opportunity for God to bless us with more. Oftentimes, we cannot be our best on our own, but we need to surround ourselves with people who can help make us better. We need to surround ourselves with people who can help us achieve a purpose in life larger than mating. Our time will come to explore God's love in the form of a Godly man. Until then, let's focus on things within our power.

The question is not why did it happen to me but how can I move forward?

When bad stuff happens we all want to know why. Why us? Were we not enough, where did it all go wrong? We ask so many questions that sometimes the thought of never understanding can make us depressed and want to give up. This feeling is natural. The way to cope in a time of chaos is not to ask why, but how. How do we move forward from this? How do we let go of the hurt and disappointment? How can we encourage ourselves? How do we forgive? How can we love, hope or wish again?

Remember, victims ask why, victors ask how. The moment you start asking how is half the battle. God is ready to take us the rest of the way if we trust him and let him guide us. No tears tonight. Your victory is already won.

STOP trying to prove to them what they could have had and focus on what you can have by putting the same time and energy into creating a better you.

The goal is not to prove to them that you are doing good without them and with someone else. The goal is not to be successful so they know what they could've had. The goal is not to beat them at their own game so they finally realize their loss. THE GOAL IS TO BE THE BEST YOU FOR YOU, for your purpose, for those looking to you to succeed and for God's glory. If that person didn't realize what they had when they had it then they definitely won't have the capacity to understand who you can be or who you will be. To be brutally honest, many of our exes won't care. Don't waste your energy looking back when those behind you don't care where you're going. Let them go. You'll be better for it.

Fear can destroy your potential for greatness. Don't let it.

Don't be more afraid than willing to change, improve yourself or move forward in progress. You were made for more. Staying where you are is not an option. If where you are right now is the same place as you were a year ago or 3 months ago, it is unacceptable. You have to want more for yourself. You have to know that you are worthy of the best future possible and that future starts today. Take control of your life. Take control of your heart. Don't be afraid of uncertainty. Don't let fear hold you back. Your potential is pulling you out of your comfort zone. Just let it happen. You'll be better for it.

Don't have to settle for less or be jealous of what someone else has. All you must do is stay focused, stay faithful and prepare for what's to come.

Jealousy doesn't pay the bills or get you what you want any sooner. Jealousy complicates things and destroys things and creates bitterness and envy which will eat you alive if you let them. But just because someone else has what you THINK you want, it doesn't mean you have to settle for who you have. At some point we have to love ourselves enough to say, I'd rather be alone than with trash. That sounds harsh, huh? Well sometimes you have to be real with yourself. When you get to the point you'd rather be by yourself than the wrong person, that's when we allow God to do his job and send to us the one we've been waiting on. Settling is never the answer no matter how stable of a lifestyle they can provide. The question is will you be happy. If the answer is no, then wait on God and stay focused on you. Your time is coming.

> Lord surround me with people who genuinely care about my well-being and do not just assume I am okay.

Sometimes with a break up you should also leave behind the friends who enabled your bad habits of running back to him, the ones who never told you the truth about your actions, and the ones who encouraged you that he was the best you were going to find. If these were your friends, ask yourself if you could do better. At times, it can be better for you to be alone than for you to be surrounded by the wrong people, the type of people who aren't looking out for you and can't help you to be better. Support is key to letting go. You need people who can remind you of the pain you walked away from and who can encourage you to keep going. You don't have to do this alone and if you don't want to, then ask God to surround you with the ones he selects just for you. He'll do it.

Starting today, no more giving up. Instead, I will learn to give God my all until I get everything that I have been praying for.

Be encouraged that even if you have to walk away from your friends, your old lifestyle and your failed relationship all at once, you are going to be okay. There are so many women who are living proof of God's grace and kindness. There are many women who are evidence of God's ability to do the unthinkable and give you a man that trusts in God's power just the same. Keep fighting, beautiful queen. Keep trusting, keep believing and keep working on you. Your day is coming.

Chapter 5
EMBRACING THE WAIT

Waiting for that special someone in life doesn't literally mean wait on the couch until Prince Charming walks through your front door. Be active, be social, be informed, be passionate, be healthy, and be better today than you were yesterday. Prepare yourself to be the best you can be. Your best will always be more attractive.

Let's be productive in our wait. As long as we have breath in our bodies, we must be grateful for the opportunity to trust in God more and more to act on our behalf. He sees our desires and he knows what our hearts long for. He has someone special for us but he just wants to be sure we trust him to do his part. Not only does he want us to trust him to give us what we are praying for, but he also wants us to be faithful even after we receive our blessing. When He blesses us with the answer we have been waiting on, we will realize how much love he put into creating a beautiful someone just for us. Don't worry, your time is coming. Just be you in the meantime.

She said WAITING was for losers yet she was the one who was lost in his empty promises, his web of secrets and his beautiful lies.

Ladies, everyone doesn't have the courage or the patience to wait on God's best for them, but don't let them tell you not to wait. Do what you're doing because you have faith in God will provide, not because someone you respect is doing it or because your friends bet you couldn't do it. It's your decision. You make the choice. Don't listen to the people who judge your improvement process with insults and harsh criticism. It takes hard work and commitment to be better, to be different and to be more than who you were yesterday. Those who have experienced an intentional change in their life know the struggle and the determination it takes to empower one's self and be their own standard. The people who condemn and mock, they have their own issues they need to work out and just need to bring someone down to feel good about themselves. Don't be the one who gives them exactly what they want. Live above the drama. Set a new standard.

Her heart waits to be the wife he deserves.

Although we are all queens, queen status does not always equal "ready to be a wife" status. We have to admit in our time of waiting, married or single, we all have some things we need to work on. Transparency is key to creating a better version of ourselves. Life is not about pretending to be someone you are not. It's not about hiding who you are until you find someone you trust enough to show them who you are. Life is about living boldly and proudly in your skin and trusting that the people who reject you are not people you need in your circle. Life is about finding genuine people in your community who value what you have to offer. But if you don't know what we have to offer, know who you are or appreciate yourself for journey you've traveled, you need to spend more time learning to love you. Until you love, accept and appreciate who you are, you don't need a husband. A husband's responsibility is not to define who you are or tell you that you should think of yourself. Their job is to remind you at times of the positive things about you that you lose sight of.

> **H**er heart waits for the man who is eager to work through their problems out sooner than later.

Problems that remain a problem for longer than they have to are draining and require unnecessary energy. It is stressful being the only person in your relationship seeking to reconcile. Settling for someone who refuses to seek solutions together and in a timely manner is not on my list of wants. I want someone who says "Babe, I was wrong" or "Babe, I know I was upset earlier, but how can we fix this" or "I don't want to go to sleep mad, so let's just work this out". My prayer is for the Lord to bless us with someone who is eager to work out problems with us sooner rather than later. Every relationship has its issues but every issue doesn't have to be the center of the relationship.

Her heart waits for an assertive man who has a soft spot just for her.

A lot of times there is a misconception that women want a push over, a weak man or someone who only lives for their woman and has no other interests in life. For me that's not true. I still want a strong man that leads, that's assertive, that's productive, that's a dreamer and that is passionate about something other than me. I simply require that he has a soft spot for me and in that space he chooses to love, me and cater to me, and to provide for me and listen to me. I don't desire to change him. I just desire that he has a special love just for me.

Her heart waits for the man who will welcome ALL the love she has to give.

Ladies, some men won't know how to accept ALL the love you have to give, but one man will. The question is are we willing to wait?

Moment of Reflection:
Are you willing to wait?

_____

_____

_____

_____

_____

_____

_____

Her heart waits for the real deal.

I don't want a cliché, a man who does things just for show or because he saw another man doing it. I want him to want me for me. I want him to cater to me because he wants to, not because he feels obligated to. I want him to want to love me and not just entertain me because it's what men do. I want something real, something dependable, sporadic yet consistent. I want him to take me seriously but still have a sense of humor. I want him to motivate and teach me new things about life without making me feel less than. He may have his flaws but I want him to trust me enough to work through them with me. He doesn't have to be perfect, I just want him to be real.

Her heart waits to love again because she knows that her last love won't be her last love and that real love is on its way.

Real love is on its way but will we wait for it? Will we be ready for it? Will we be "worthy" of (meaning are we protecting our value or are we still giving it away)? Patience is key to receiving everything you've been praying for but you have to remember to make room for your blessings because otherwise you might miss it. Let's get rid of the distractions and things that only temporarily satisfy us. Let's know our worth and protect it because someone is on their way to claim it. Gods timing may be different for you than someone else, but his timing is perfect. Don't lose faith. His vision of your future is more than you can even comprehend. Sleep well tonight.

Her heart waits for the moment she realizes that every sacrifice that she's ever made was all worth it.

Do you feel like you are wasting time and that your prayers are not being answered? Listen up. If your heart is in the right place and your faith is activated, every sacrifice you've made has all been for a reason. Believe it and let that encourage you when things get tough. Every tear you've cried, every heart ache and every thought of foolishness you've had is about to be eased by the realization that the one you've been praying for exists and that God was preparing him for you all along. Stay strong for just a little while longer.

Her heart waits on God to say, "I made this one for you."

This day would make me so happy.

Moment of Reflection:
How would hearing these words make you feel?

_____
_____
_____
_____
_____
_____
_____
_____
_____
_____
_____

Chapter 6
A MOMENT OF DOUBT

Sometimes the closure you think you need just re-opens the wounds that have already been closed.

They say "leave well enough alone", and that is the truth. Sometimes you go searching for answers or searching for closure all just to end up lessening your self-respect in the process. If you already know you're not going back and there is nothing anyone can say to change your mind, why put yourself in tempting positions that force you to compromise your growth. Your purpose is bigger than you can imagine and you have to protect it. You're doing just fine where you are, but you have to love yourself enough to protect your testimony because someone is waiting to hear it. You have to protect your heart from places you know aren't best for you. You have to make the decision and stick to it. Your future depends on it. Be encouraged

I was considering going back but then returned my memory.

We can't choose to forget the bad stuff when it's convenient for us and when loneliness begins to sit in. Although the past is in the past, it still happened and our reason for leaving then isn't any less valid now. We gotta stick to the story that motivated us to walk away in the first place. Selective memory is the worst thing you can have when you're vulnerable. Be strong and keep moving forward. Know that the only thing behind us is the past, which will get repeated if we walk back into it. Be smart, be safe and be a better you. You are worth so much more.

"Selective memory is the worst thing you can have when you're vulnerable"

The only thing behind you is the past, which will get repeated if you walk back into it.

I know what it's like to want to go back to something that's comfortable, even if it wasn't always good, it's still familiar. I know that sacrificing the one you thought you loved for someone who will love you right in the future almost seems impossible, especially when the one you want starts to be the man you wanted him to be. Choosing to move forward is a hard decision, and although many people give in, we ALL have the power to stay strong and continue on. God sees your fight for his promise and if you keep fighting, he will not deny it to you. You are worthy of so much more than you can imagine. In due season.

I know it's hard to see right now, but that person who walked out of your life did you a favor.

Sometimes we want to blame our failures on the people who walked out on us not realizing the misery that we may have had to endure if they stayed. Some people may say I'd rather have a man around who doesn't love than not one at all. Or they might say that I'd rather have my biological parents around than the people who raised me and loved me right. Others might say they don't care why someone left them, but all they know is that they will never forgive their absence.

Listen up! When people walk out of your life, it's a reflection of them. It's a reflection of who they are, what they want and how much of life they can handle. It's a personal decision that you can't change and therefore you need not beat yourself up about it. You can only control you. You can only love you and regardless of how bad it hurts; you have to look forward. You have to find the blessing in the pain. You have to find the beauty in the chaos and you have to understand that whatever happens in this life is meant to shape you into your very best self.

It's so true that what doesn't destroy you makes you stronger. And what's even more true is that sometimes people are doing you a favor when they walk away because that's them getting out of the way and letting God do His business in your life. Don't fear, God is here and He's going to help you get through this.

"Be encouraged"

You might think you want to go back but ask yourself who you will be 6 months, 1 year, or 10 years from now. Do you like what you see?

You may feel like this fight for God's best will never be over but I'm here to help you think about what will happen if you give up now. If you give up now eventually the pain you feel now is going to be ten times worse. Your need for God's love will be ten times greater. Going back to what hurt you should be hard, but for many of us it is so easy *especially* when love is involved. Can I tell you something? If you are struggling to walk away from what's behind you because you know there's better in front of you, then what you felt wasn't love. It was an imitation of love. It may have looked like love and felt like it, but the truth was revealed about it the moment it walked out of your life. Real love is unconditional, it leaves you with memories of joy and life lessons. The thought of it makes you want to be better. If all you can think of is the negative that's going to be in your life if you back to what used to be, then why return? Why settle for an imitation of love when you can have the real thing? Patience.

You could go back but then all your progress would be worth less.

Are you sleeping in the right place tonight? Don't go back, stay on track to discovering a better you. Your future is depending it.

Moment of Reflection:
Are you willing to wait?

_____
_____
_____
_____
_____
_____
_____
_____

Resist the devil and he will flee from you.

The Bible says to submit to God, resist the devil and he will flee from you. What does this mean? It means if we resist the urge to do wrong when we are faced with temptation then we take away the enemy's power over our lives. It means that if we choose to do right even when every part of us wants to satisfy a temporary need, then the enemy loses his power to influence us. When the devil flees from us, it is because he loses and the God within us is stronger than the enemy thought. I'll tell you a secret. God is always greater and God always wins. He just wants us to access him and he will fight for us. Don't give in to temptation and get set back especially when God is setting you up for greatness. You got this.

Why settle for an imitation of love when God wants to give you the real thing?

Many of us have only ever really felt real love from our parents, family or people in our community when we were younger. As we have gotten older, we have sought to duplicate that feeling in men but we find that real love cannot be forced, it just is. It is the same way that God just is. Real love makes us better and it makes our hearts full. It reveals the greatness within us and it protects our spirit from hurt, hate, discouragement and negativity. It's the kind of love that helps us to feel that, no matter what life faces hands us we will be okay.

God's love for us is the prime example of that love. His love is the standard and his greatest gift to us. Not only does he want us to know his love but he wants to give us a double dose. He wants to bless us with the one he prepared for us, the one who is greater than our most vivid imagination. God's only requirement is that we seek him first in our pursuit for love and that we trust he will fulfill his promise. When we go searching for quick fixes and booty calls, we will never find the love that God wants to give us. When we try to force what God has not sent, the best we will receive is an imitation of love. Because God is an awesome God, he can turn that imitation into the real thing, but if that person is not willing to learn to love you right, then what? Don't settle. The time we spend chasing an imitation is not worth the time we lose receiving God's best for us.

"Real love makes us better and it makes our hearts full."

Listen up! You are somebody's blessing in the making and if you give up now not only could they miss out on their blessing but you could miss on someone special.

Sometimes your process is not just about and what you need but it's also for you to become the perfect fit to what someone else needs. You may doubt that God knows what he's doing because it's taking a little longer than you would like but I assure you that He does. He knows what he's doing and all of His work is for your benefit. Never forget that God honors those to believe in His almighty ability to do the impossible. Keep your faith. Know that your wait is not hopeless and that in due season, your wait will be only a memory because God will have done exactly what He does best and that is to give you the life better than the one you imagine.

Chapter 7
ENCOURAGE YOUR YOURSELF

You were created for more so go out there and get what's yours.

There's nothing wrong with waiting for what's yours! You don't have to settle for less or be jealous of what someone has! All you have to do is stay focused, stay faithful and prepare yourself for what's to come. Discover your passion, go after your dreams, live productively and when you least expect it, doors will open and opportunities will follow. You got this, just wait on it.

> **"I will STOP living for him and START living for me because when it's all said and done, I am responsible for the choices I make and the life I live."**

We have to take responsibility for the bad choices and take credit for the good ones, but nonetheless, we must own them. We are responsible for ourselves and if we keep allowing ourselves to blame others then we are going to continue to struggle. If we don't see our own faults, we will continue to let others drag us down. We will let others continue to have control of our freedom if we don't learn to stand up and say, no matter the consequence, I take full responsibility. Our lives are our own, and our faith should be in God's ability to see the intentions in our hearts and to make us new. We don't need to depend on a man to accept us or to like us. We just need to focus on being a better version of who we are, someone closer to who God has called us to be. We can do this.

Sometimes you have to tell your situation.

"I AM NOT THE ONE. I WILL NOT LOSE MY FAITH. I WILL NOT BE DEFEATED. IT'S MY SEASON. I WILL WIN."

It's your life, take control of it. It's your season and you will win. You will not doubt. You will not fear. You will not lose your faith but you will trust. You will believe and you will be triumphant. No worries, no fears, just victory. You have to claim your victory, because it's yours!

Despite everything I have been though, I still have to say thank you for allowing me to be where I am and for giving me a future to look forward to.

We have to be grateful for the things that seem small to us now so God can bless us with our biggest dream. If we are faithful in saying thank you now, we won't forget who blesses us with more. God wants to bless us and he also wants the glory. Stay faithful.

"Your best is yet to come."

Lord, today I am expecting a miracle.

Lord, today we are expecting a miracle. We ask that you have your way in us and give us the eyes to see your glory manifested today. Lord we give you full control to let your will be done and we will not allow fear or doubt to keep us from receiving what's in your will for us. We step aside, Lord.

Moment of Reflection:
Are you willing to wait?

I realize that I would rather be alone than in a toxic relationship. I love myself too much for that.

I love myself too much to keep experiencing unnecessary pain. I may go backwards sometimes and I may fall sometimes, but each time I pull myself back up, I gain a little more strength inside of me to do better the next time.

Toxic relationships destroy your self-esteem, your pride, your spirit, sometimes friendships and possibly even your finances. They make you feel empty and unworthy and deep down you know that you deserve better than that. Fight for your future and your sanity. Understand that you are beautiful and so worthy. You deserve God's best for you. You're not a slave to toxic relationships but you have the freedom to walk away and live your life in peace. Learn to love on you today and be encouraged.

The enemy is trying to shake me but my faith will not waver.

The enemy can be so ruthless and it will try to steal your joy the moment you find peace within yourself. It wants you to crawl in a corner and hide and the moment you give in, he wins. Don't let the devil steal your peace and place fear in your heart. Know that our God is bigger, stronger, wiser and higher than any other. No weapon formed against us shall prosper. The Lord is a jealous God and he will not tolerate those who attempt to bring harm to his children. Keep your faith up. For those who have accepted his son, Jesus, God has got us in his hands. Remember that

𝐈 will not doubt God's ability to do the IMPOSSIBLE. I've come too far to let the enemy steal my FAITH.

I will not lose faith, not today. I've come too far. I've worked too hard. I prayed so much. I have let go of people I love. I have lost respect that took years to earn. I have accepted that I will not be that person anymore. I want to be more and I can be more. I will not lose sight of the future you have created for me. I will trust you. "Lord, keep me where you want me. Remind me that I am yours and what I am fighting for."

"You have come too far."

He's an on time God.

He may not come when you want him, but he'll be there right on time. Don't lose your faith. Stay focused and stay strong. You are not alone and God sees you.

Name 5 times God has provided a way for you when it initially seemed like there was no way.

1. _____
2. _____
3. _____
4. _____
5. _____

Not only will you be my good thing, but you will be even better than the best version of you that I could have ever imagined.

In due season.

Moment of Reflection:
Are you willing to wait?

_____
_____
_____
_____
_____
_____
_____

Chapter 8
YOU'VE GOT THIS

Forget about whether or not THEY like you. When you look in the mirror, do YOU like you?

This is the real question.

Moment of Reflection:
Do you like you?

_____

_____

_____

_____

_____

_____

_____

_____

_____

_____

_____

Know who you are and know who you are not.

Self-love is all about loving you for you. That means being confident in who you are and knowing who you are and who you are not and who you refuse to be. When you do not know who you are, you will answer to anything and that is unacceptable. Continue to love on you, you'll figure it out. Stay encouraged.

There is no beauty in wearing a mask of lies just so people won't see your scars.

We all want people to think we are always the best version of ourselves. This is why we always tell people we are fine and only share the good in our lives and not our struggle. The truth is we all struggle and there's nothing attractive about being that single person on the earth with no problems. No one is perfect, so we have to stop pretending to be. We are beautiful flaws and all. The sooner we realize we can live beautiful, honest, imperfect lives that represent who we truly are. It's a great day to be great. Stay blessed.

"No one is perfect, so we have to stop pretending to be."

There is strength in your story, don't be afraid to tell it.

Sometimes our truths hurt and remind us of our poor judgments but we can't let embarrassment keep us from sharing our story. Not only will we find the strength to go on by telling our story, but others will find the strength to keep fighting by knowing they are not the only ones going through heartbreak, hard times or headaches. We all struggle and we all fall short, but it is our responsibility to keep moving forward. It is our responsibility to encourage those around us. It is our responsibility to help each other stand up after a fall. We can't be great alone. It takes community, transparency, and honesty to let go. Remember who you are and remember that your story is meant to be told. Remember you are stronger than you think and never forget your life is bigger than you. You got this. Stay strong.

Don't just SURVIVE the season you're in, but THRIVE in the season you're in. God has you here for a reason.

This is a lesson I'm learning more and more each day. Surviving is doing what you have to do to get by until something better comes along and makes your situation less uncomfortable. Thriving is when you make the most of what you have and are content with where you're at yet eager to see what's next. Living in survival mode implies you are living in fear that you won't have enough and that is not God's desire for us. He wants us to know He will provide and He can be our everything. In Him we have more than enough. No matter what season we are in, He is MORE than enough. Be encouraged, our best is yet to come.

Don't wait until you're in a relationship to begin working on you. Improve now and avoid the petty stuff later.

Prepare now to avoid the problems that would arise later, for example, sharing, communication, consistency, meaning what you say, discipline, productivity, learning how not to tell your friends all of your business, etc. Granted, there will always be problems because that's life, but why not avoid the petty stuff if you can. Just my thoughts.

"Preparation is essential."

Love when you're ready, not when you're lonely and not before you learn to love yourself.

Sometimes we want to be loved so badly we forget to ask ourselves if we are ready for it. Maybe you have plans to further your career now, graduate without children, travel with friends, learn a new craft or pursue a passion that requires a serious time commitment. Are you ready to love you, work on developing you and pursue a future with someone else? It's okay if you are not. Rushing love when you're not ready for it can leave you can you still feel lonely due to bad timing. Focus on creating a better you for a second. Self-love attracts true love. Remember that.

The best thing you can do for yourself is to learn to love who are you are, unapologetically.

You don't have to trust me. Try it for one week and notice the empowerment you feel in your life. Notice the change in attitude and the amount of peace that consumes you. When you discover who you are and become that person unapologetically, you tap into true confidence and it's that true confidence which unleashes the ultimate mark of beauty.

Moment of Reflection:

Do you have what it takes to be unapologetically you?

_____

_____

_____

We can't rush what we want to last forever.

Patience is key. No matter how much we want what we want right now, we have to remember that waiting is a process. A process takes time. A masterpiece takes time. God is creating a masterpiece of our lives that people will awe over. People will see our lives and ask how. How is it that you two found each other? How is it that your love seems so effortless? The questions will start coming and there will be one answer, God. God does all good things in his timing and if we want what's good, we understand the value of waiting, we just have to do it. Be encouraged. One day at a time.

You are enough.

Before God can use you, he has to deliver you from your own insecurities, helping you to realize that you are enough. Sometimes he even has to deliver us from insecurities we don't even know we have. Know this, there are no limits on God and He wants to use you right where you are, but we have to be willing to see that He can use us just the way we are. If we are enough for God, all other opinions don't matter. Remember this and let no one convince you otherwise.

"You are enough!"

Chapter 9
MY PLEDGE

Dear Reader,

    You've made it to the last page in our journey together and this is where you continue on putting into practice the wisdom you gained from page one. From here you make the choice every day not to lose sight of the future that's in front of you, to prioritize you and you choose to live the abundant life that you are worthy of. There will be no looking back. There will be no fear or shame in starting over. This is your season!

    Below, you have the opportunity to make this commitment to yourself. This commitment can also be an affirmation that you say to yourself every morning, every night, every time you feel doubtful or every once in a while. Your signature symbolizes a promise that you are making to yourself to never settle and to be your best you. This is a serious commitment and one that can change your life forever.

Peace and Blessings,

Cioré Taylor

Cioré Taylor

My Pledge

"I pledge to never forget that I am worthy, I am never alone and I am enough. I am loved by the one who matters most and forgiven by the one who matters most. I cannot change my past, but I can raise my expectation for my future. I am beautiful, I am wanted, I am confident and someone's blessing. I will not allow my poor choices or my mistakes to define me because I know God defines me. He says that I am beautifully and wonderfully made and that He will do abundantly beyond anything I can ask of Him in my life and I choose to believe Him. I will believe what He says about me and when I doubt Him, I will deny that fear any power in my life. I will not force love. I will not fight my heart when it says no. I will not settle for any man who doesn't value me or treat me right. I will be patient and I will focus on creating the best version of me while waiting on God's best for me. I can do this."

Signature: _____
Date: _____

HER HEART WAITS

What is Her Heart Waits and what does it stand for?

Her Heart Waits is a women's ministry devoted to restoring faith, productivity and hope in women to desire more in life. As young women, many of us grow up wanting nothing more than to fall in love with Prince Charming and live happily ever after. The problem is many of us do not lead productive lives as we wait to be found. We also tend to misplace our faith in men when God is the one who provides all of our needs now and forever more. Her Heart Waits seeks to empower women to take responsibility for their own lives and to avoid placing the blame on others. My mission is that every woman has the confidence and tools to unapologetically say "I will create the best version of me while waiting on God best for me."